The U.S. Army, Navy, and Air Force Medals of Honor (left to right) are unique in their design. Marine Corps and Coast Guard members receive the Navy medal.

Recipients of the Medal of Honor have distinguished themselves through conspicuous "gallantry and intrepidity" at the risk of their lives, "above and beyond the call of duty."

Congress created the Medal of Honor during the early years of the Civil War. Since then, about 3,500 individuals have been awarded the Medal of Honor.

Candidates are nominated by their commanders, and at least two eyewitnesses must attest to the candidate's actions. There is an extensive review and vetting process. When the honor is granted, the president bestows the medal in a ceremony at the White House. The award honors those who put aside their fear and fight to preserve freedom and to protect their fellow soldiers, airmen, seamen, and marines in all theaters of war—often against overwhelming odds.

THE MEDAL OF HONOR SERIES

by Michael P. Spradlin

JACK MONTGOMERY

World War II: Gallantry at Anzio

RYAN PITTS

Afghanistan: A Firefight in the Mountains of Wanat

MEDAL OF HONOR

Jack Montgomery

Jack Montgomery

World War II:

Gallantry at Anzio

MICHAEL P. SPRADLIN

FARRAR STRAUS GIROUX
NEW YORK

Farrar Straus Giroux Books for Young Readers
An imprint of Macmillan Publishing Group, LLC
175 Fifth Avenue, New York, NY 10010

Text copyright © 2019 by Michael P. Spradlin
Maps copyright © 2019 by Gene Thorpe, Cartographic Concepts, Inc.
Printed in the United States of America
by LSC Communications, Crawfordsville, Indiana
Designed by Eileen Gilshian and Cassie Gonzales
First edition, 2019
Hardcover: 10 9 8 7 6 5 4 3 2 1
Paperback: 10 9 8 7 6 5 4 3 2 1

mackids.com

Library of Congress Cataloging-in-Publication Data

Names: Spradlin, Michael P., author.
Title: Jack Montgomery : World War II : gallantry at Anzio / Michael P. Spradlin.
Other titles: Jack Montgomery, World War II gallantry at Anzio
Description: First edition. | New York, NY : Farrar, Straus Giroux, [2019] | Series: Medal
   of Honor ; 1 | Includes bibliographical references and index. | Audience: Ages 8–12.
Identifiers: LCCN 2018019099| ISBN 9781250157065 (hardcover) | ISBN
   9781250157072 (pbk.) | ISBN 9781250157089 (ebook)
Subjects: LCSH: Montgomery, Jack, 1917–2002—Juvenile literature. | Anzio, Battle of,
   Anzio, Italy, 1944—Juvenile literature. | United States. Army. Infantry Division,
   45th—Biography—Juvenile literature. | Soldiers—United States—Biography—
   Juvenile literature. | World War, 1939–1945—Campaigns—Italy—Juvenile
   literature. | World War, 1939–1945—Participation, Indian. | Indian soldiers—
   Biography—Juvenile literature. | Cherokee Indians—Biography—Juvenile
   literature. | Oklahoma—Biography—Juvenile literature.
Classification: LCC D763.I82 A558 2019 | DDC 940.54/215092 [B]—dc23
LC record available at https://lccn.loc.gov/2018019099

Our books may be purchased in bulk for promotional, educational, or business
use. Please contact your local bookseller or the Macmillan Corporate and Premium
Sales Department at (800) 221-7945, ext. 5442, or by email at
MacmillanSpecialMarkets@macmillan.com.

Dedicated to the men and women of the U.S. military,
past and present, who keep our country free

CONTENTS

U.S. ARMY RANKS

Partial list, from lowest to highest

Private
Specialist
Corporal
Sergeant
Staff Sergeant
First Sergeant
Command Sergeant Major
Second Lieutenant
First Lieutenant
Captain
Major
Lieutenant Colonel
Colonel
Brigadier General
Major General
Lieutenant General
General

The ranks corporal through command sergeant major are noncommissioned officers. They are enlisted soldiers who rose through the ranks and don't have a commission. Commissioned officers—second lieutenants on up— generally have a college degree. They are often graduates of a military academy or a university's Reserve Officers' Training Corps program. In World War II, to replace officers lost in combat, enlisted men showing exceptional leadership were given battlefield commissions and promoted to second lieutenant. Commissioned officers who began their military careers as enlisted soldiers are referred to as Mustangs.

U.S. ARMY UNITS AND SIZES

Army Unit and Size	Number of Soldiers	Commanding Officer
Field Army = 2 or more Corps	50,000–250,000	Four-Star General
Corps = 2–5 Divisions	20,000–45,000	Three-Star Lieutenant General
Division = 3–4 Brigades	10,000–15,000	Two-Star Major General
Brigade/Regiment* = 3–5 Battalions	3,000–5,000	Colonel
Battalion/Regiment* = 4–6 Companies	200–1,000	Lieutenant Colonel
Company = 3–4 Platoons	50–200	Captain
Platoon = 3–4 Squads	15–40	Lieutenant
Squad = 10 Soldiers	10	Staff Sergeant

The number of soldiers in each unit varies depending on where it is deployed, its mission, and the available personnel, or individual unit strength.

* Before 1957, regiments were brigade-level units of about three thousand men, containing three battalions, artillery, and other supporting units, commanded by a colonel. Since then, the army has largely eliminated regiments as a command unit, with a few exceptions. Special Forces, Rangers, and armored cavalry still use brigade-level regiments, while today some army airborne units comprise battalion-level regiments commanded by a lieutenant colonel.

Jack Montgomery

Campaigns of the 45th Infantry Division

July 1943–April 1945

GERMANY

BELG.

Frankfurt

Paris

Strasbourg

Central Europe *Mar.–Apr. 1945*

CZECH.

Dachau

Rhineland *Sept. 1944–Mar. 1945*

Munich

SWITZ.

AUSTRIA

HUNG.

Lyon

FRANCE

Venice

ITALY

Adriatic Sea

YUGOSLAVIA

Marseille

Hotel Campo Imperatore

Gustav Line

← **Amphibious landing**

Southern France *Aug.–Sept. 1944*

Rome

Naples

← **Route of advance**

Axis controlled as of July 1943

Anzio–Rome *Jan.–June 1944*

Anzio

Salerno

Salerno *Sept. 1943–Jan. 1944*

Mediterranean Sea

Algiers

Tunis

Messina

SICILY

Ionian Sea

Miles

0   100   200   300

Scoglitti

Map by Gene Thorp

ALGERIA

Sicily, *July 1943* **45th Infantry Division**

STEPPING ASHORE

Anzio, Italy
January 30, 1944

LIEUTENANT JACK CLEVELAND MONTGOMERY LED HIS
platoon through the icy-cold knee-deep seawater toward
the beach. As he did, he thought about the way things
worked in the U.S. Army—how the decisions of where
and when to fight were made. The generals never asked
the guys on the ground, the platoon leaders like him,
for their opinions. They just gave the orders. He sure
wished they'd asked this time. In private conversations,
most every one of his fellow officers wondered about
this battle plan. They said it made no sense. It was too
rushed. They had air support and plenty of troops, but
a lot was missing to ensure a successful mission.

First was the lack of critical intelligence. Which divisions of the German army were facing them? How much infantry? Artillery? How many paratroopers?

German forces had been chased out of Sicily—the large Mediterranean island just off the "toe" of boot-shaped Italy—and were scrambling to get into position to hold the Italian Peninsula. The Italians had already surrendered, their air force shot out of the sky. Did the Luftwaffe—the German air force—have pilots and planes ready to attack? No one knew exactly what was ahead.

The Germans were concentrating their defenses along the Gustav Line, which stretched roughly a hundred miles across the narrowest part of the Italian Peninsula. Thousands of soldiers manned machine guns and artillery in trenches and concrete fortifications across the mountains. Planted with land mines and strung with barbed wire, this defensive position blocked the most logical and direct route from the south to Rome, the capital of Italy.

The officers of the U.S. landing forces understood that Adolf Hitler, the German führer, was incensed at how quickly the Italian army had folded after the Allies showed up. If he didn't divert German troops to slow the enemy's advance north through Italy, the Allies

Propaganda poster from the Soviet Union promoting the effort to defeat Hitler

HITLER VS. THE ALLIES

Adolf Hitler (1889–1945) and his Nazi Party rose to power in Germany in the 1930s. In 1933, he became Germany's chancellor and soon established an absolute dictatorship, holding control over the entire German state. He remained in power by eliminating all other political parties, controlling the military, and imprisoning or executing his opponents.

The Allies were the countries who had banded together to defeat Hitler, including Britain, France, Australia, Canada, New Zealand, India, the Soviet Union, China, and the United States of America.

could march right up to Berlin, the German capital, or invade southern France, which his forces occupied.

Hitler already had his hands full with the Soviet army in the east, which was turning back his invasion of the Soviet Union. He was also fortifying the northern coast of France, believing the Allies would launch an invasion from across the English Channel. To say the führer was in a bit of a tizzy would be a vast understatement.

Jack Montgomery had fought with the Allied forces a few months earlier as they cut through Sicily like a sharp knife through cheese. He had earned a battlefield commission and was promoted from sergeant to second lieutenant. Now they had sailed around the Gustav Line, and Rome was within their reach. Still it wasn't going to be easy. It never was. Lieutenant Montgomery and his men had no idea they would end up fighting some of the Nazis' most battle-hardened troops.

The second problem, and the most critical for an infantryman as far as Lieutenant Montgomery was concerned, was that they were going ashore with almost thirty-six thousand troops but without nearly enough armor. His Thunderbirds—the 45th Infantry, with about 1,500 Native American soldiers—were landing behind the German lines. Only one division of armor was attached to the operation, providing limited tanks and not enough heavy artillery for ground fire support. Not good. Not good at all. Without enough armor, infantrymen like Montgomery and his platoon didn't tend to last long in a fight.

In truth, this was how the army worked. When leaders saw an opportunity, they took it. Sure, the generals studied maps and intelligence briefings, discussed the best way to deploy their forces, and made plans. But most of the time it was a "ready or not" approach. If they thought they had a chance to land behind enemy lines and punch Hitler in the kisser, they took it, whether or not they had the right number of troops, ships, equipment, or whatever. And they didn't give two hoots and a holler about what a lieutenant in the infantry thought about their plans. Especially when the lieutenant was a Cherokee who belonged to a National Guard regiment. His opinions went to the back of the line. It was his job to fight when he was told to. The army wasn't interested in his suggestions.

"Dang, this water's cold," he heard a voice behind him say.

"It ain't gonna get any warmer from all yer hot air," a no-nonsense sergeant groused.

American soldiers storming the beach during the landing at Anzio

The soldiers of his platoon trudged through the water in full gear, packs weighed down with ammunition and rations. Lieutenant Montgomery could tell his men were nervous and scared. Stumbling along, suffocated by equipment so heavy they could barely move, they could almost feel the German guns pointed at them.

That was another thing that bothered Montgomery.

There weren't enough landing craft. Instead, many troops rode in small boats as close to the shore as they could, and then waded the rest of the way. The whole operation felt rushed from the start. With a landing craft, you at least had a fighting chance. It could drive right up on the beach with its machine guns blazing, giving you covering fire. The ramp lowered, and you ran out of it like a fox chasing a hen until you found cover.

Sometimes the bullets flew so thick you swore you could walk on them. Then the tiniest piece of cover would do. A small dip in the sand, a piece of driftwood. Anything that made you feel like it would offer even the smallest amount of protection. The only thing Montgomery couldn't understand was, here they were, wading ashore, and there was no resistance. No German or Italian machine guns or artillery attempting to halt their advance. At least not yet.

He didn't like it. Not one bit. Had they somehow surprised the Germans? Were they expecting the Allies to land someplace else?

The platoon finally reached the shallows, and Montgomery and his team splashed ashore. The usually incessant German shelling had momentarily ceased. Montgomery and his men had been ordered in as reinforcements for an offensive taking place a few miles inland. So far, Allied air power had been unable to knock out the German guns waiting to greet the invaders.

Montgomery studied the terrain around them. Far off in the distance he could see rocky mountain ranges. They were covered in thick woods. If he were the Germans, scrambling to get into position to defend against the invasion, that's where he'd go. He wouldn't like it, but he would concede the beach and concentrate his forces on the high ground. It was classic military strategy. Always take the high ground; facing an enemy from above gave you the advantage.

Montgomery looked back toward the beach. What days ago had been empty shoreline now teemed with tents, vehicles, and army personnel. Farther off, on the blue water of the Mediterranean Sea, dozens of Allied ships of all sizes bobbed on the waves. Compared to what they had gone through in Sicily, this landing had gone smoothly.

Too smoothly.

Hearing a low whistling sound, Montgomery returned his gaze to the distant mountains. It grew louder, heading straight for them. It was the unmistakable hum of an artillery shell. It was soon joined in chorus by dozens of others.

"Incoming!" someone shouted.

Montgomery's platoon scrambled to haul their gear and take whatever cover they could find. The world around them exploded in noise and fire.

The Germans had just announced their presence

with authority. Montgomery knew instantly this wasn't going to be like Sicily. They wouldn't be facing poorly trained and ill-equipped Italian troops that had already given up.

"Everybody dig in!" he shouted. "I guess they know we're here."

AN ATHLETE GOES TO WAR

JACK CLEVELAND MONTGOMERY WAS BORN NEAR LONG, Oklahoma, on July 23, 1917. He grew up on a farm in Sequoyah County, just west of the Arkansas border, where thousands of Cherokees had resettled in the 1830s after the U.S. government forcibly removed them from their lands in the southeastern United States. Their forced march to Oklahoma came to be known as the Trail of Tears.

Montgomery's mother was Cherokee, and at age thirteen he and his three sisters attended Chilocco Indian Agricultural School, a boarding school run by the federal government. He was an outstanding athlete. "There

The 1909 Chilocco Indian Agricultural School basketball team. The swastika on the uniform was a common Native American symbol of good luck long before it became associated with the Nazi Party in Germany.

were maybe three or four hundred students in the school. I started in the seventh grade and stayed throughout my sophomore year," Montgomery said. (In an interesting coincidence for such a small school, another

Chilocco student, Ernest Childers, would also be awarded the Medal of Honor in World War II.)

In eleventh grade, he attended public high school in Carnegie, Oklahoma, where he lettered in basketball and football. Classmates described Montgomery as a kind, humorous, and outgoing young man. He "showed great determination to finish what he started," according to one. His football prowess earned him a scholarship to Bacone College, in Muskogee, a college that catered to Native American students.

While Montgomery was a student at Bacone, he enrolled in the Oklahoma National Guard, joining I Company of the 180th Infantry Regiment in 1937. The company was composed almost entirely of Native American students from Bacone. It was a way to make a little extra money during the Great Depression.

Living in Oklahoma in the 1930s was not easy for farming families like Jack Montgomery's. America was in the middle of the worst economic disaster in U.S. history. More than 20 percent of the nation's population was unemployed. Oklahoma was very hard hit. The state was experiencing a prolonged drought, which killed the crops and dried up the top layer of dirt where crops grow and flourish. Winds swept the exposed

A farmer and his sons walking in the face of an Oklahoma dust storm, April 1936

topsoil away in gigantic dust storms across the Great Plains, and prairieland in Kansas, Colorado, Oklahoma, Texas, and New Mexico became known as the Dust Bowl. Farmers lost all their land and money. Oklahoma's agricultural industry nearly died.

These "black blizzards" sometimes traveled all the way to the East Coast. Circumstances were so bad that the Dust Bowl became a nationwide obsession.

Newspapers ran front-page stories on the Oklahomans' plight. Movie theaters showed newsreels of the horrible conditions.

Thousands of starving, desperate Oklahomans abandoned the state and headed to California, looking for greater opportunity. It was one of the biggest voluntary mass migrations in American history. Those who left became known as Okies. Some of Jack Montgomery's family left in beat-up trucks and old cars, or in any transportation they could find, riding on freight trains or hitchhiking. So many people traveled to California along U.S. Route 66 that author John Steinbeck dubbed it "the mother road, the road of flight" in *The Grapes of Wrath*, his 1939 novel about the plight of a poor farming family.

In 1938, Montgomery headed to California, too. After he earned his associate's degree at Bacone, he accepted a scholarship to the University of Redlands. There he continued to star on the football field and cemented his legend for toughness.

During one Redlands game in famed Rose Bowl Stadium, a player on the opposing team burst through the Redlands defensive line and was on his way to an easy touchdown. Only one thing stood in his way. Number twenty-two, Jack C. Montgomery. Montgomery tackled the ball carrier so hard that he left the man unconscious. The crowd was stunned, and one woman is said to have remarked, "Did that little ole boy knock out that great big man?"

Montgomery earned a bachelor's degree in physical education in 1940, but with no place to go after graduation, he returned to Oklahoma. He looked for a job as a teacher or a coach but found he lacked the proper educational credits to teach. So he rejoined his old National Guard unit, completed his required year of service, and was discharged as a sergeant in September 1941.

America was finally emerging from the Great Depression, but the rest of the world was in turmoil. Japan had invaded China in 1937, destroying everything in its path as it marched through the countryside. Millions of Chinese citizens were killed during the onslaught. Japan was now looking to expand its empire southward and become the dominant power in the Pacific.

In Europe, in 1939, Hitler had launched his blitzkrieg, or "lightning war," in Poland. Indeed, the Germans were the first to use this tactic of striking targets quickly and without mercy. In a blitzkrieg, Germans would

THE RISE OF THE NAZIS

In this propaganda poster, a Nazi dagger stabs a snake with a Star of David on its head. The snake is labeled with such terms as usury, unemployment, Marxism, lies, corruption, white slavery, terror, *and* civil war. *The Nazis blamed Jews for all of Germany's problems.*

In 1919 Adolf Hitler joined the small German Workers' Party, the forerunner of the Nazis, at a meeting in a Munich beer hall. In 1923 Hitler and his Nazi Party attempted to overthrow the German government and failed. He was tried for treason and sent to jail. While locked up for nine months, he wrote a book that outlined his vision for Germany to take its place as a global superpower through national socialism. National socialism stresses the obedience of the citizen to the government in all matters, emphasizes inequality of the races, and asserts the right of the strong to rule the weak.

Through a relentless propaganda campaign in

posters, newspapers, and rallies, the Nazis grew in popularity, and Hitler found a national audience. He promised to make Germany into a powerful nation and to take back lands he believed rightfully belonged to the German people. He opposed communism and believed that the Soviet Union, as a communist state, posed a serious threat to German security.

When the Nazis won the most votes of any party in the 1932 elections, Hitler demanded he be made chancellor. He was appointed in 1933, and when the nominal president died in 1934, Hitler declared himself führer, or leader.

As Hitler gained power over the everyday lives of German citizens, he implemented a plan to "purify" the German race. The Nazis stripped Jews of their German citizenship and prohibited them from marrying German citizens. The state-sponsored racism would ultimately force all Jews and other minorities into concentration camps.

The world saw Hitler as a looming threat as he ordered conscription into the military and ramped up the German industrial base to build planes, tanks, ships, and submarines. But the world did nothing when he took over German-speaking Austria and parts of Czechoslovakia. That changed when Germany invaded Poland in September 1939 and crushed the Polish army in one swift blow.

concentrate planes, tanks, and artillery on a narrow front and drive a breach into the country's defenses. Armored tanks would quickly penetrate and drive freely behind the lines, causing chaos and disorganization. German planes would prevent any reinforcements, and soon opposing troops would be encircled and forced to surrender. Poland, Denmark, Norway, Belgium, the Netherlands, Luxembourg, and France all fell to these maneuvers and the might of the German army.

In July 1940, the German Luftwaffe began almost *daily bombing runs on Great Britain* to prepare for an invasion. The raids would go on for three months in an attempt to break the will of the nation. However, the British people and especially the Royal Air Force refused to give in during the Battle of Britain.

No matter how many attacks the Germans launched, British fighter pilots of the Royal Air Force turned them back. Running short on fuel, planes, and supplies, the RAF pilots would fly mission after mission, taking time only to grab a quick meal while landing and refueling their aircraft before taking off to fight again.

British bomber pilots were not idle. As Germany attacked, Britain retaliated, increasing its own bombing runs on important targets in territory the Germans

Hitler reviews German troops during the invasion of Poland, September 1939

had recently conquered, such as submarine bases and strategic ports along the coast of France. The Royal Air Force was outmanned and outgunned, but with the support of the British people and the encouragement of their leader, Prime Minister Winston Churchill, the RAF fought the Germans to a stalemate, forcing Hitler to abandon his invasion plans.

This was the world Jack C. Montgomery found himself in when his enlistment in the National Guard ended in September 1941. There was no doubt the United States was gearing up for war, but the country was still divided. Many citizens wanted America to enter the war to help our allies, especially in Europe. Others were drastically opposed to any involvement.

London children whose homes have been destroyed during the German bombing, 1940. Over a million children were evacuated from British cities that year, moved to rural areas away from their parents where there was less risk of aerial bombardment.

But soon came an event that changed everything. It united the country in a way it has seldom been, before or since. It caused Jack C. Montgomery to reenlist.

Early in the morning of December 7, 1941, Japan bombed the U.S. naval base at Pearl Harbor in Hawaii, using over 350 aircraft in a surprise attack. Thousands of American sailors, soldiers, and marines died. Hundreds of airplanes were damaged or destroyed, and all the battleships in port were targeted. Two were completely lost.

Pearl Harbor naval base in Hawaii under attack, December 7, 1941

The next day President Franklin Roosevelt asked Congress for a declaration of war against Japan. His request was granted. Days later, Japan's allies in the Axis, Italy and Germany, declared war on the United States.

Like it or not, America was at war—as was much of the rest of the world.

DIGGING IN

Anzio, Italy
January 30, 1944

TREES EXPLODED CLOSE TO THE ALLIED POSITIONS. THE
impact of the shells was so powerful that the trees were
obliterated, instantly turning into thousands of tiny
wooden projectiles. When soldiers were injured, they
were sent to an aid station. These stations were located
on the beach, behind the Allied lines.

Soldiers returning from the aid stations would remark on how heavy the shelling was at the rear. Many
men asked not to be sent to the rear, even if they were
wounded. They felt safer on the front.

The artillery barrage was unrelenting. German artillery hurled shells from up to eighteen miles away. As

Lieutenant Montgomery thought, they had chosen their defensive positions well. They were dug in, hidden in the hills, and it gave them a huge advantage.

The enemy wasn't the only challenge facing Lieutenant Montgomery and his platoon. Many problems were created by the nature of the war itself. British and American soldiers made up the bulk of the Allied forces. This meant that leaders from both sides wanted to have a say in plotting military strategy, allocating the troops and resources, and deciding the priorities and plan of attack.

The invasion of Italy was the first time since the start of the war that American troops had landed on the European continent. Adolf Hitler, after conquering so much territory, boasted that he had created Fortress Europe and no Allied troops would ever dare set foot on European soil again. Now his boast was nothing more than hollow words.

Allied troops first fought together in North Africa, where they faced German forces under the command of Field Marshal Erwin Rommel. Known as the Desert Fox, Rommel led the German forces to great success on the battlefield. When the Americans arrived, a quick victory eluded them. Their army was largely made up of recently activated National Guard units and fresh

Allied troops landing in North Africa

recruits. The German troops were combat trained and far more experienced.

General Eisenhower selected General George Patton to command the armored forces in North Africa. Patton had modernized the American armor divisions and was as brilliant at tank warfare as Rommel. Under the Allied command structure, however, Patton had to answer to a British general, who also oversaw General Bernard Montgomery, the British commander who had been fighting Rommel for six months. It was an uneasy arrangement.

The British generals didn't trust the Americans' fighting ability, and Patton chafed at the limited role his troops were given. Together, though, the Americans and British pushed Axis forces out of North Africa and captured Rommel's crack troops.

From there the Allies set their sights on Sicily, which the Germans and Italians were using as a base to control the Mediterranean Sea. The Allies' timing was perfect. The Italian leadership was crumbling. Two weeks after the Allied forces landed in Sicily in July 1943,

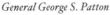
General George S. Patton

the Italian dictator Benito Mussolini, one of Hitler's closest confederates, was toppled from power by his own government.

The Allies were on the offensive. Their attack in Sicily sent shock waves throughout Europe. Now Adolf Hitler was faced with the prospect of an attack from the south. His armies were busy fighting in Russia and preparing to defend against an expected invasion of Allied

Allies on the move in Sicily

troops in France. He was forced to divert more precious resources, men, and supplies to Italy.

If Sicily could be secured, the Allied leaders were not in agreement about what to do next. Victory in Sicily would mean that shipping lanes in the Mediterranean were under their control. If this happened, the Americans wanted to devote all their resources to Operation Overlord (now commonly called D-Day) the following year.

After success in Sicily, the British, especially Prime Minister Winston Churchill, badly wanted to push up the Peninsula and capture Rome. Churchill believed a continued assault would tie up German resources, making the upcoming D-Day invasion easier. If the Allies took Rome, they would send a signal to the world that Hitler was reeling and on the defensive. It would be a huge morale boost to the troops as well as to British and U.S. citizens.

The decision the Allies ultimately made nearly led to disaster for soldiers like Lieutenant Montgomery and his men. While President Roosevelt, Prime Minister Churchill, General Dwight Eisenhower, and other leaders played politics, they sent their armies into a battle with inadequate equipment, an indecisive plan, and poor leadership.

Mussolini and Hitler, 1940

DOWNFALL OF A DICTATOR

Like Hitler, Benito Mussolini served in World War I, and he returned to Italy as a right-wing nationalist. Mussolini insisted his country needed a ruthless dictator to deal with Italy's postwar problems and suggested that he was the man. Soon he had a militant following, and the fascist movement was born.

In 1922, when armed fascist militias marched on Rome, the Italian king made Mussolini prime minister. Mussolini ruled under the constitution until 1925, when he put it aside and made himself dictator, or *Il Duce.*

Early on, Hitler admired Mussolini. The two shared similar political philosophies and imperial desires. Hitler actively encouraged Mussolini's invasion of Ethiopia in 1935 as the rest of Europe expressed its horror. They soon formed the Rome-Berlin Axis.

Mussolini understood that Italy could not stand alone against Western powers like Britain and the United States, and he wanted a share of Hitler's spoils. But after using Italian forces to occupy Ethiopia and to support fascists in Spain, Mussolini did not have the resources to wage more war. When he sent troops to fight Britain and France in North Africa, the Italians suffered so many losses that Hitler had to send Rommel to the rescue.

The Italians also suffered defeats in Greece and the Soviet Union. Bombing raids, first by the British and later the Americans, took a toll on citizens at home. The country was demoralized, and the army was weary. Mussolini's own fascist ministers stripped him of power on July 24, 1943, and the Italian king had him arrested and put in prison.

ATTACK OF THE THUNDERBIRDS

LIEUTENANT JACK C. MONTGOMERY WAS PART OF THE 45th Infantry Division of the United States Army. It started as a National Guard unit from the American Southwest and included many Native Americans from Arizona, New Mexico, Colorado, and Oklahoma.

Before the United States entered World War II in 1941, the country did not have a large standing professional military. In 1940, only about four hundred thousand men served in the army and navy, making it the eighteenth largest military in the world. However, each state had its own National Guard, controlled by the governor. During natural disasters or civil unrest such as

U.S. National Guard recruiting poster from World War I

riots or strikes, the National Guard was often deployed to keep order and help rescue victims. When necessary, the U.S. government could "federalize" National Guard units, temporarily making them a part of the U.S. military.

The 45th Division became known as the Thunderbird Division because its insignia was a thunderbird, a powerful spirit in the form of a bird that holds tremendous importance in the lore of many of America's native peoples. Depicted in yellow on a red background, the thunderbird made a distinctive shoulder patch on the uniform and was a tremendous source of pride.

Jack Montgomery was proud to be a part of the Thunderbirds. When he rejoined the division after the attack on Pearl Harbor, he knew many of the men in his company from his previous stint in the unit. It was good to be going to war with familiar faces. The division's motto was *Semper Anticus*, Latin for "always forward." Men like Montgomery lived by the motto. "All of them were good soldiers, dependable," he said. "If you went forward and said to somebody, 'Cover me,' you never looked back."

Montgomery returned to the unit as a sergeant. He reported to Fort Sill, Oklahoma, where the 45th Division was sent to begin basic combat training.

Morale in the Thunderbirds was strong. "In the Forty-Fifth there wasn't any problem between the Indians and the whites," Montgomery later said. "In 1941, I Company of the 180th regiment was an entirely Indian company that consisted of students from Bacone College . . . The captain was white, and the first lieutenant was an Indian. In 1941, there were five Indian sergeants in I Company, 180th, that got direct commissions."

FROM SWASTIKA TO THUNDERBIRD

When it was originally organized in 1923, the 45th Division used an ancient symbol of good luck—the swastika—as its insignia. It was a common symbol of prosperity or well-being in many ancient cultures, including the Greeks and the Hindus. In 1920, Hitler chose the swastika as the Nazis' symbol, and it has been associated with them ever since.

The 45th Division needed a new symbol. The division held a contest to find a design, and a panel of officers eventually settled on the thunderbird. For many Native Americans, the thunderbird is a great figure of power and strength. It is celebrated in art and song especially among the tribes of the Great Plains, the Northwest, and the Northeast. Since the 45th Division included men from over fifty Native American nations, the thunderbird was the perfect symbol. The new insignia was approved by the War Department in 1939 and has become one of the most famous insignias in U.S. Army history.

Soldiers from the 45th Division on a troop ship bound for North Africa,
June 1943

Training continued in Camp Barkeley, Texas, and then the division was sent to Fort Devens, Massachusetts, where the 45th trained in amphibious warfare. The Thunderbirds got a taste of winter in Pine Camp, New York, before they were posted to Camp Pickett, Virginia. The division took part in combat maneuvers in the Blue

Ridge Mountains and practiced amphibious landings in the Chesapeake Bay while waiting for orders to deploy.

Those orders finally came, and on June 8, 1943, the Thunderbirds set sail. They reached North Africa on June 22. Allied forces there had finally defeated and corralled the Germans in May. While awaiting their next next orders, Sergeant Montgomery and his men practiced more amphibious assaults.

By now the Thunderbirds were well trained. The amphibious assault practice was especially important. The men of the 45th Division would be landing on beaches swarming with German troops prepared to drive them back into the sea. Throughout history, armies had carried men and supplies by water to land for an attack. But the world had never seen amphibious assaults on this scale before.

The training itself was dangerous. The landing craft sometimes ran aground short of the beach. They could be swamped in the waves. Men were carrying heavy packs and equipment. If they stumbled and fell in the water, the weight of their equipment could pin them under the water. Accidental drownings were not uncommon.

Finally, the Thunderbirds learned the news. On

Soldiers inside a landing craft sheltering from enemy fire. This image was taken during the D-Day invasion in June 1944.

July 10, 1943, the 45th Division would put its training to the test. It had been decided. The U.S., British, and Canadian troops would launch an amphibious attack on Sicily.

Sergeant Jack Montgomery would get his first taste of combat.

It would be a treacherous landing. The Germans were expected to put up a ferocious defense.

But no one, not even Jack Montgomery, knew yet that the Germans had fallen into a trap that helped pave the way to an Allied victory. It was a brilliant deception, planned and executed by British military intelligence.

A SPY STORY

England
1943

BEFORE THE INVASION OF SICILY TOOK PLACE, BRITISH
intelligence officers created an elaborate ruse to hide
the location of the attack. It involved a number of carefully created false papers, a dead body, and the man who
would go on to create James Bond. It was called Operation
Mincemeat.

This deception was an exercise in counterintelligence.
It was a highly delicate and complicated plan to fool
Germany into believing the Allies would attack near
Greece in the eastern Mediterranean. If Adolf Hitler
and his generals could be fooled into believing this lie,
they would be forced to move troops and equipment from

Sicily, and it would be much easier for the Allies to take the island. The island would give the Allies control of vital shipping lanes. Since most men and materials were moved by ship, it would be a huge tactical advantage in the war.

The concept for Operation Mincemeat came from an idea suggested in 1939 by Ian Fleming, an assistant to the head of British Naval Intelligence. More than a decade before he would publish his first novel about Agent 007, Fleming was doing his part for the war effort. It was his job to help develop counterintelligence plans. One idea, he wrote to his superiors, was based on a hoax he had read in a detective story:

> *A corpse dressed as an airman, with dispatches in his pockets, could be dropped on the coast, supposedly from a parachute that had failed. I understand there is no difficulty in obtaining corpses at the Naval Hospital, but, of course, it would have to be a fresh one.*

In early 1943 a plan inspired by this idea was put into motion. It involved creating an elaborate false identity and putting the corpse where the enemy would find it. The body would carry letters and misleading documents

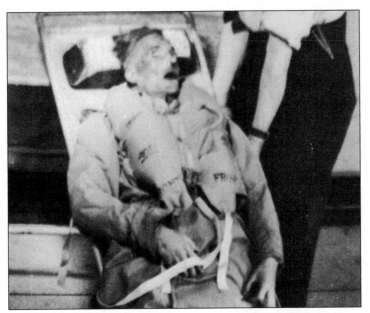

The body of Glyndwr Michael was transformed into Major William Martin of the Royal Marines.

about plans for an Allied invasion. The falsehood would require careful preparation, not only of the documents but of the body itself. It might come from one of England's hospitals or morgues. The body would need to be carefully preserved. If there was too much decomposition, enemy medical experts might become suspicious.

The body of a deceased Welsh day laborer named Glyndwr Michael seemed a suitable corpse. While MI5, the British Security Service, prepared the documents, the body was stored in a refrigerator. A fake identity was created, and Glyndwr Michael became Major William

Martin of the Royal Marines. His identification papers showed him to be attached to the Royal Admiralty.

Carefully constructed letters were written and put in a briefcase handcuffed to his wrist. Fictitious personal notes were carried in his uniform pockets, one from his father and the other from a girlfriend, to match the picture of her he carried in his wallet. The "official" letters were written by various officers to commanders in North Africa. They held hidden but easy-to-decipher clues about the next planned invasion, and they all said it would take place in Greece as part of a larger Allied plan to take the Balkans.

The biggest problem was how to make sure the body got into German hands. Again, British counter-intelligence was ready. In 1941, the British had decrypted Germany's Enigma code, which allowed them to decipher radio transmissions and learn what the Germans were discussing and planning. British intelligence knew that Spain, which claimed to be neutral in the war, was in truth collaborating with Nazi Germany. So the decision was made to drop the body off the shores of Spain. If Spanish officials found the body convincing, they would turn the papers over to the Germans for inspection.

The Trojan horse

THE STRATEGY OF DECEPTION

The use of deception in warfare is as old as warfare itself. A famous example is the Trojan horse, supposedly used by the Greeks as they battled the Trojans for a city named Troy more than three thousand years ago. According to the story, after a long, unsuccessful attack against Troy, the Greeks constructed a giant, hollow wooden horse and hid their elite warriors inside. The rest of the Greek army sailed away.

Thinking they had won a great victory, the Trojans pulled the horse inside the city gates as a trophy. That night, the Greek warriors climbed out. They overpowered the guards and opened the city gates for the rest of the Greek army, which had sailed back under cover of darkness. The Greeks destroyed the city and won the war.

Deception was routinely practiced in World War II. Both sides created fake tanks, airplanes, and other vehicles out of balloons, wood, and canvas, positioning them in plain sight. From the air, they looked real and caused the enemy to overestimate how much armor or supplies a force possessed.

On D-Day, the Allies used planes, dummy parachutists, and small ships to simulate an invasion force headed toward the French city of Calais, two hundred miles north of the real Normandy landings. Dropping thin strips of aluminum in the air, the planes created false radar echoes that made it seem as if a large fleet was underway.

A U.S. soldier with an inflatable tank

On April 30, 1943, a sardine fisherman found the body floating off the shore of Huelva, Spain. Authorities were called, and the Spaniards and Germans took the bait. The documents were passed all the way up to Hitler. He moved troops and equipment to reinforce his positions in Greece and the Balkans. His generals, and the Italian dictator Mussolini, failed to convince him that Sicily was the logical place for the Allies to attack.

The briefcase was eventually returned to the British naval attaché in Spain, who sent it back to England. To completely sell the fake plan, the British sent an unencrypted cable back, saying that experts had examined the envelopes and found no evidence of tampering. The attaché was instructed to express Britain's deepest appreciation for the care the Spaniards took and was permitted to tell them in confidence that one of the documents was of utmost importance. The naval attaché was in on the ruse, of course, and a second, secret cable informed him that the letters had indeed been opened. He casually spread the word that the British believed the envelopes had not been tampered with, knowing this falsehood would reach German ears.

Glyndwr Michael, a poor, homeless laborer, was buried in Huelva, Spain. His tombstone credits his service as MAJOR WILLIAM MARTIN, RM. His role in deceiving the German high command was instrumental in the triumph of the Sicily invasion.

Operation Mincemeat was a total success.

THE INVASION OF SICILY

Scoglitti, Sicily
July 10, 1943,
before dawn

SEVEN MONTHS BEFORE JACK MONTGOMERY AND THE
Thunderbirds splashed ashore on the beaches of Anzio
on the Italian mainland, they were landing on Sicily,
the largest island in the Mediterranean. Code-named
Operation Husky, the Allied attack on the Italian territory was a massive invasion: one hundred fifty thousand soldiers, three thousand ships, and four thousand
aircraft.

General George S. Patton commanded the U.S.
forces, and General Bernard Montgomery led the British troops. The invasion force landed on the southern
shores of Sicily—a hilly island about the size of Vermont,

dominated on the northeast by Mount Etna, at eleven thousand feet the highest active volcano in Europe.

In a brilliant stroke of strategy, the Allied commanders went through with the invasion despite gale-force winds that whipped up high seas during the night. The German and Italian defenders figured there was little possibility of an enemy landing in such horrible weather. But the first assault waves hit the beaches before dawn. They found little resistance. It wasn't just the high seas that kept their opponents' forces unprepared. The success of Operation Mincemeat had resulted in the removal of large numbers of German troops and armor. The Axis forces were waiting for the Allies to attack in Greece. With the seas so rough, the initial landing had caught the remaining German and Italian troops by surprise.

The high seas and rolling swells particularly affected Jack Montgomery's 180th Regiment. Landing teams were scattered across twelve miles, when their planned landing zone was supposed to be less than two miles long. This left two of the regiment's battalions disorganized and undermanned when they faced the only serious opposition to the landings; the 180th lost thirty lives, more than half the Allied soldiers who died on Sicily that day.

Allied beachhead on Sicily, July 10, 1943

By that afternoon all one hundred fifty thousand Allied troops were ashore, along with six hundred tanks. It was the first amphibious landing by the Allies in Europe since the start of the war.

When an army establishes a beachhead, it tends to look chaotic. From a distance, it seems as if an anthill has suddenly erupted in the sand: thousands of scurrying invaders—not to mention trucks, tanks, and other equipment—are scattered everywhere. In this case, the tension for the majority of the Allied attackers was heightened as they had expected heavy resistance. When that didn't happen, they worried about where the Germans were hiding.

From the beaches near Scoglitti, the 45th Division

rolled inland in the coming days, capturing the towns of Vittoria and Ragusa. Part of its assignment was to take the airfields at Comiso and Biscari. With hundreds of planes and huge stores of ammunition, the airfields were important strategic targets.

At Biscari the 180th Regiment encountered stiff resistance. The airfield was crawling with Germans. Snipers and machine gunners in the grounded aircraft turned their weapons on the approaching invaders. The Allied forces, led by the 45th, took control of the airfield—but not before the German and Italian forces regrouped and launched a violent counterattack. The fighting was intense, but the enemy forces were finally repelled.

From the airfield onward, fighting was nearly nonstop. The 45th was up against the Hermann Göring Panzer Division. Göring was one of Hitler's most trusted military advisers. The troops were well trained and would not be defeated easily.

Over the next few weeks the forward progress of the 45th was arduous. Much of the fighting was close combat, sometimes hand to hand, with Germans and American soldiers grappling amid the rocks and dirt. When ammunition ran out, they used knives and entrenching

Soldiers of the Hermann Göring Panzer Division man a machine gun on Sicily, July 1943.

tools as weapons. An officer in the 45th Division recalled seeing one of his men battering a German soldier with his helmet.

Inch by bloody inch, the 45th Division clawed northward. The number of casualties mounted as the Thunderbirds fought their way across the volcanic island. Before long, Sergeant Montgomery found himself in charge of the platoon as other commanders were wounded or killed in action. For the next few months, he was right in the thick of the fighting.

"I took charge of the platoon for the rest of the campaign in Sicily," he said. "When it was over, they recommended me for a battlefield commission. I got it the day before we went to Salerno."

Montgomery was promoted to second lieutenant. The conduct of Montgomery and the men of the 45th Division pushed the German and Italian troops off Sicily. It was a major victory and, as in North Africa, took conquered territory away from Adolf Hitler and Nazi Germany.

General George S. Patton singled out the 45th Division with special praise. "The Forty-Fifth Division, a green outfit, went into combat with two veteran outfits, and asked for no favors, made no excuses. They kept up with the other outfits. I'm . . . proud of every officer and man in the division."

In little over a month, the Allies drove the Axis forces off Sicily. On August 17, 1943, when the Allies reached the port of Messina at the northern tip of the island, less than two miles from the Italian mainland, they discovered that the Germans had pulled thousands of soldiers across the water, reinforcing their positions for the Allied invasion they now knew was coming.

For their victory on Sicily, the Allies paid a heavy cost. Nearly thirty thousand soldiers were killed or wounded.

Italian soldiers taken prisoner after the Allied landing in Sicily

A FORMIDABLE FORCE

During the Sicily campaign, the 45th Division proved to be a formidable fighting force despite its inexperience. Over the first five days of fighting, the 45th Division captured substantial Axis resources:

15,000 small arms (rifles and pistols)

10 million rounds of ammunition

700 machine guns

38 artillery pieces

49 trucks

160 aircraft

44 tanks

222,000 gallons of fuel

5,000 soldiers

A wounded U.S. soldier receives plasma from a medic in Sicily on August 9, 1943.

But Jack Montgomery and the Thunderbirds had been tested. They were up to the task. The experience they gained on Sicily's rocky shores would serve them well in the coming fight at Anzio.

FROM SALERNO TO ANZIO

September 1943–
January 1944

WITH A COMPLETE VICTORY IN SICILY, THE ALLIES
turned to mainland Italy. But the invasion did not happen easily. Over the preceding months, the United
States and its allies could not agree on the proper course
of action.

British Prime Minister Winston Churchill desperately wanted a follow-up invasion of the mainland. The
United States was looking ahead to the invasion of
France in the spring of 1944. Churchill believed that the
time to strike "the soft underbelly of Europe" was now.
Doing so would force Hitler to respond by bringing
more troops and supplies to Italy. It would also force

TRENCH FOOT

An army hygiene poster

One of the biggest problems facing armies in the field is disease and illness. In fact, in many cases, more fatalities have been caused by sickness than by injuries inflicted on the battlefield. One illness that has caused armies trouble is trench foot.

As soldiers march or camp in damp areas, their feet become wet. The prolonged exposure to damp conditions can cause pain, swelling, and numbness in the feet, leading to serious blisters and infection. In severe cases, tissue dies and falls off.

Trench foot was a serious issue in World War I, which was fought in trenches throughout the European countryside. The trenches would fill with water, and the permanent dampness led to trench foot.

At Anzio, the area near the beachhead was surrounded by swamps and marshes. When soldiers dug foxholes, water would seep in. The weeks and months the soldiers spent in the damp fortifications created the perfect conditions for trench foot.

Soldiers had to dry their feet each day and change socks regularly. They were paired with partners to check each other's feet. To keep their feet out of the water, they would try to find wood and other materials to line the bottom of the fox-holes.

him to pull troops from France, where they expected an Allied invasion, or from the Soviet Union, where the Soviet army had started to beat back the German invaders, causing them to retreat.

Though they agreed that Hitler had overextended himself, the United States was reluctant to land on mainland Italy. There were a number of reasons why.

First were the several hundred thousand German troops already in Italy. The sixty-five thousand soldiers who managed to escape the Allies in Sicily now reinforced the mainland German positions.

Second was the problem of geography. Away from the coastal areas, the terrain in southern Italy is rugged and mountainous. In wintry conditions, this terrain is even more challenging.

Third were the lessons from Italy's own history. Many times over the centuries, the Italian Peninsula had been overrun by invaders. But successful invasions of Italy did not come from the sea. They originated from the north and came through the mountain passes of the Italian Alps. Even the great general Hannibal chose to attack by land in 218 B.C. rather than take the direct route across the

In 218 B.C. the Carthaginian general Hannibal invaded Italy from the north, crossing the Alps. He famously used elephants as part of his army.

sea from Carthage in North Africa. As Napoleon is said to have advised, "Italy is shaped like a boot. And it must be entered the same way. From the top."

Italy's hilly interior gives defenders too much of an advantage. Invaders trying to attack from the sea would be exposed on the flat coastal plains. Defenders could set up their artillery on the high ground a few miles inland and hurl shell after shell at any forces attempting to land on the coast. The attackers would be sitting ducks.

In spite of the danger, Churchill pressured the U.S. commanders to strike and sent pleas to President Roosevelt. Churchill was desperate to capture Rome. Doing so, he believed, would further undermine the Axis alliance of Germany, Italy, and Japan. On the other side of the world, in the Pacific war against the Japanese, U.S. forces were retaking island after island and driving the Japanese back toward their homeland. By capturing the Eternal City of Rome, Churchill knew the Allies would send a message to the world that the Axis powers had been weakened in Europe as well.

The arguments went back and forth. One factor tipped the scales in Churchill's favor. Since the 1920s, Italy had been under the control of dictator Benito Mussolini. For years, Mussolini had been a key ally of Adolf

Hitler. While the Italian army was not well trained or equipped as a fighting force, the Axis partnership with Mussolini gave Hitler a buffer to his south and access to the shipping lanes in the Mediterranean Sea.

But as the Allies made headway in Sicily, the political situation in Italy was thrown into chaos. Mussolini's fascist ministers stripped him of his powers, allowing King Victor Emmanuel to remove him as prime minister. Mussolini was arrested and imprisoned in an isolated ski resort in northern Italy. The new prime minister secretly sent word to the Allied forces that he wished to negotiate a truce. Italy formally surrendered to the Allied powers on September 3, 1943.

But that summer, even before the armistice with Italy, as fortune seemed to be favoring the Allies on Sicily, U.S. military leaders were finally in agreement with the other Allies to proceed with an invasion of mainland Italy. The secret armistice with the new government in Rome was an important step. As the Allies planned to invade mainland Italy, they wanted to reduce the number of opposing forces.

On September 3, after the Italians surrendered, British forces crossed the Strait of Messina from Sicily into mainland Italy. Six days later the 45th Division made

German commandos snatched Mussolini from an out-of-season ski resort with a Storch (stork) light aircraft, specially designed for short takeoffs and landings.

THE RESCUE OF MUSSOLINI

Hitler was enraged by the situation in Italy in 1943, including the arrest of Mussolini. In September, he sent a team of SS commandos to free *Il Duce* from his isolated location, a ski resort in the Italian Alps. In a daring raid by air, without a shot being fired, the commandos rescued the Italian dictator from his confinement and brought him to Germany.

the first U.S. landings on mainland Italy near Salerno. They encountered heavy resistance from German troops and heavy armor as they thrust inland.

The brutal fighting went on for weeks. It was during this campaign that Jack Montgomery earned a Silver Star, the third-highest decoration for bravery in combat.

"I was supposed to set up this roadblock about two

miles in front of where the rest of the battalion was. The last order was that the battalion and the regiment were going to move forward at daylight and the British were supposed to be on our right flank. When it got daylight, we saw the crossroads and the Germans that were holding it. We were up above them and we opened fire," Montgomery said.

"We surprised them completely. For about fifteen or twenty minutes, we had a big firefight. We only had about two or three people wounded; they were able to walk out. We found out later from the Italians around there that there were about two hundred German troops in the area, and we were almost completely surrounded. I didn't know that then. But we surprised them so much that they took off."

Fighting continued through December before reinforcements arrived and the exhausted troops were pulled back to Salerno from the front lines after seventy-two days of continuous combat. They had pushed the Germans a hundred miles back through mountainous terrain and treacherous weather.

The Germans were entrenched in the mountains of Italy along the Gustav Line. They had established artillery positions. And they were reinforced by the nearly sixty-five thousand troops that had retreated from Sicily.

Once again, the Allies debated the next step in the invasion of Italy. Winston Churchill pushed hard for capturing Rome, the capital city. General Patton and General Eisenhower argued that Rome held little strategic value.

In the end, the decision was made to launch Operation Shingle and land Allied forces *behind* enemy lines at Anzio. Allied planners decided the Italian seaside resort of Anzio was an ideal geographical option for an amphibious attack, seventy-five miles north of the heavily fortified Gustav Line. The wide beaches with shallow approaches would allow the landing craft to make it onto shore easily. The roads out of Anzio would give immediate access to the main thoroughfares leading to Rome, about thirty miles north. An Anzio landing would also draw German troops away from the Gustav Line, which another Allied force would try to breach as well.

The Allied forces took the Germans completely by surprise at Anzio. Enemy guns stayed eerily silent. One private reported, "It ain't right, all right. But I like it."

By the night of January 22, 1944, thirty-six thousand

soldiers had come ashore. But instead of driving inland with the element of surprise on his side, the Allied commander chose to build up his supplies and only cautiously pushed a few miles inland. This decision would come back to haunt the Allies, as it allowed the Germans to bring up reinforcements. The Germans had rapidly dispatched units south from Rome and several more from Yugoslavia, France, and Germany. In the coming days the fighting grew fierce, with the Allies unable to get off the beachhead.

The Germans would surround the Allied forces and pin them down for four months with nearly continuous

The Anzio landing, January 1944

shelling. Both sides would take heavy casualties as the Allies tried to fight their way out.

The delay and subsequent stalemate caused Winston Churchill to remark, "I had hoped that we were hurling a wildcat onto the shore, but all we had got was a stranded whale."

The Thunderbirds' 180th Regiment with Lieutenant Jack C. Montgomery landed at Anzio on January 30.

As always, an amphibious landing was fraught with peril, and by now the Germans were regularly shelling and strafing the area. Nat Crandall, a private assigned to the 180th, described what it was like to ride a landing craft onto the beach during an amphibious landing. "The LST had a flat open deck and a superstructure for crew and controls on one side. My friend, Ernie Friedman, and I were positioned in the shade of the superstructure watching huge geysers of water shoot skyward. We didn't yet realize that we were being shelled by what later became famously known as the Anzio Express—a very large-caliber cannon mounted on a rail flat car that receded into a tunnel in the mountain when attacked by the Allied Air Force. The explosions were enormous."

Despite their own reinforcements, the Allies lost momentum. What followed was an ugly, vicious style of

Alongside a canal near Anzio, U.S. soldiers take a break in front of their sandbagged foxholes.

war, similar to the trench warfare of World War I. The Thunderbirds dug in, living for weeks at a time in foxholes and trenches. The area around them was marshy and damp, and the foxholes often filled with water. In addition to the Germans, disease became another enemy. A condition known as trench foot sent many soldiers to the rear.

The Germans attacked with aerial bombings, artillery, and ground troops, but neither side could gain any advantage. Lieutenant Jack Montgomery's platoon slowly reduced in number. Their fellow soldiers were wounded, fell ill, were captured, or were killed in action.

By February, the platoon of normally forty men was down to about twenty capable fighters. At some point, one side would have to give.

Lieutenant Montgomery and the rest of the Thunderbirds were determined not to blink. No matter how hard the Germans battered the division, the men held the line. And on a February day, Lieutenant Jack C. Montgomery would achieve his Medal of Honor moment.

"COVER ME"

Padiglione, Italy
February 22, 1944

THE FIGHTING HAD BEEN GOING ON FOR WEEKS. THE
clashing infantry units of the Allied and German forces
had blended into a long, twisting, confusing line of men
and deadly machines. German attacks were frequent
and furious. Still, Lieutenant Jack Montgomery and the
Thunderbirds of the 45th Division refused to bend.
Nothing the Germans threw at them was successful.

Both sides turned their artillery loose to full effect.
The bombardments went for hours on end. Shells landed
from all directions. The Germans unleashed their
rocket artillery, the *Nebelwerfer*. The shells fired by this

weapon made a distinctive wailing sound as they flew. The noise was so unnerving, soldiers gave them the nickname Screaming Mimis.

Both sides were taking heavy casualties. Much of the fighting happened after sundown. Many times, soldiers from one side or the other would survive an attack at night, only to find at daybreak that the lines had shifted and they were now behind the enemy. These lost soldiers hid or played dead until the darkness returned and they could try to make their way back to their units.

In the early morning of February 22, 1944, Jack Montgomery and his platoon found themselves on the tip of the Allied lines near the village of Padiglione. As the sun rose, they discovered that the Germans were close. Very close. They were dug in with four machine guns and a mortar just a short fifty yards away from Montgomery's men. Another machine-gun nest was a hundred yards away, and at three hundred yards was a house occupied by German soldiers with yet another machine gun.

As Montgomery recalled, "The terrain there was kind of flat. It was a little after daylight. My platoon was supposed to have about forty people, but we were down to about twenty. We were on I Company's left flank, and there was a road between us and the company to our left."

Montgomery analyzed the tactical situation. "There were one or two houses there that hadn't been all knocked down yet but nobody was living in them. The Germans were around one of those houses and they just got closer to us than they should have. I was looking to see where they were and what they were doing—I had no intention of doing what the army said I did."

What Jack Montgomery did next would result in his being awarded the Medal of Honor. Instructing his men

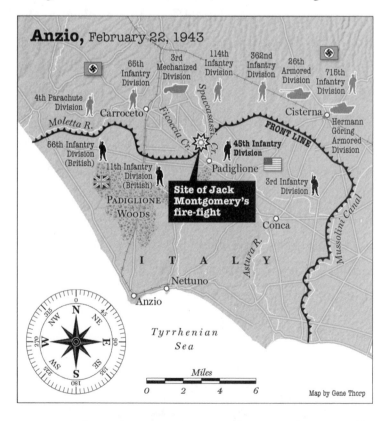

Anzio, February 22, 1943

4th Parachute Division
65th Infantry Division
3rd Mechanized Division
114th Infantry Division
362nd Infantry Division
26th Armored Division
715th Infantry Division

Carroceto
Cisterna

Moletta R.
56th Infantry Division (British)
11th Infantry Division (British)

Ficoccia Cr.
Spaccasassi Cr.
FRONT LINE

45th Infantry Division

Hermann Göring Armored Division

PADIGLIONE WOODS
Padiglione
Site of Jack Montgomery's fire-fight
3rd Infantry Division

Conca
Astura R.

I T A L Y
Mussolini Canal

Nettuno

Anzio

Tyrrhenian Sea

Miles
0   2   4   6

Map by Gene Thorp

A German machine-gun nest

to shelter behind a stone wall, he eased himself into a small ravine, crawling to within hand-grenade distance of the first machine-gun nest. "I was always going somewhere I didn't have any business going," he said later. "I told my platoon to cover me and I went out there. When you did that, you never looked back. You knew that as long as they're alive, they'll be looking out for you."

His trust in the men of his platoon and of the Thunderbird Division was absolute.

When he was in range of the closest machine gunners, he climbed on a little mound and opened fire. As the Germans fell for cover, he stood up, fully exposed, and threw his grenades, killing eight of the enemy and capturing four who surrendered.

Returning to the platoon with his prisoners, Montgomery gathered more grenades and set his sights on the second machine-gun nest. He also called for artillery fire on the house in the meantime.

Once again, his men covered him while he reentered the ditch to attack the second target. And attack it he did, killing three enemy soldiers. His gunfire was so accurate that the remaining seven Germans immediately surrendered.

Now he turned his attention to the house.

There was no ditch or other concealment in the flat open ground between him and the building. After the artillery barrage stopped, Lieutenant Montgomery ran toward the house. There was no place to hide. To him it didn't matter as he threw his grenades and laid down deadly gunfire. As German soldiers ran from the house, they threw up their hands and surrendered.

He took thirty-two prisoners that morning. There were eleven enemy dead and an unknown number of wounded. The main thing, as far as Lieutenant Montgomery was concerned, was that his platoon was safe from the withering fire of the enemy machine guns.

The men of his platoon were awestruck by what Lieutenant Montgomery had done. In safeguarding them, he had single-handedly taken out three enemy positions posing a direct threat. Montgomery had fought like a demon to protect his platoon.

That night, artillery fire from both sides started up again.

"I went over to a different company to see how they were doing," Montgomery recalled. "I was coming back alone through a big ditch when a shell hit."

Lieutenant Montgomery suffered shrapnel wounds in his left leg, right arm, and chest.

"It wasn't very long before my medic found me. I don't remember his first name, but his last name was Beadle. Your medic was one person that you had to have confidence in. I knew Beadle would find me."

Lieutenant Montgomery was taken to the shore hospital. His wounds were serious, and he was scheduled to evacuate on a medical ship to Naples. However, the ship came under fire by German gunners and left without him. Lieutenant Montgomery remained at the shore hospital. He found that experience to be much scarier than any combat he had seen.

"The hospital was just tents, and the tents had holes in them from all the enemy artillery and mortar fire. [When an attack started,] I'd roll off the cot and hit the

Anzio beach hospital tents, which were continually bombed, strafed, and shelled by German forces

floor. I told them, 'Dig me a hole here.' It wasn't long before they were digging holes for everyone. They finally sent me back to Naples."

From there, he was eventually shipped home. "When I got back to the States, it was a year and a day since I had left."

Lieutenant Jack C. Montgomery was out of the fight. But he had given his all.

Above and beyond the call of duty.

AFTERMATH

LIEUTENANT MONTGOMERY'S FIGHT WAS OVER, BUT THE war went on. The men of the Thunderbird Division would continue pressing the fight against the German army.

In the interior of Italy south of Anzio, Allied forces finally broke through the Gustav Line on May 11, 1944. They raced north toward the stalemate on the beachhead as Germans began withdrawing toward Rome. Early on the morning of May 23, the Thunderbirds, along with six other divisions on the beachhead, attacked. Two days of fierce fighting later, they were out and headed for Rome, joining up with the Allied forces from the south.

The men were glad to get out of their foxholes and be on the offensive. The 45th Division chased the enemy north. Yet the Germans' rear guard fought desperately, and some of the most bitter fighting of the entire campaign took place during their retreat. Rome fell to the Allies on June 5, 1944, the day before the D-Day invasion at Normandy in France. The 45th Division was pulled from the front and placed in reserve. Since Sicily, it had been in combat for 281 days.

The Thunderbirds' fight was not over. On August 15, 1944, the 45th Division undertook its fourth amphibious assault, landing in the South of France. The divison plowed north through the Rhône Valley as the German army fought delaying and defensive actions. The Thunderbirds occasionally ran into stiff resistance, but for much of the way they pushed the tired German army back with ease.

For several months, with only brief periods of rest, the division fought its way more than six hundred miles north through France. On March 17, 1945, the Thunderbirds entered Germany, smashing through the Siegfried Line, the fortified defensive wall that stretched along the German border from Switzerland to the Netherlands.

In April, the 45th Division was part of the Allied

U.S. troops cross the Siegfried Line into Germany, 1945.

force that liberated the Dachau concentration camp, the first of thousands of prison camps established by the Nazis. At least thirty-two thousand inmates perished at the forced-labor camp over the course of the war, and many thousands more died after passing through Dachau to Nazi extermination camps. U.S. troops were shocked at what they found. James A. Rose, an Ohio soldier from the 42nd Infantry Division, recounted: "I seen thousands of people crowding out that looked like skeletons with skin stretched on them. They were dirty, they smelled, and just one look at them, some of them half dead, something happened that we realized that this war was all about, we know now why we were participating in this war."

From there, the 45th pushed on to Munich and took that major city with plans to drive onward, but Germany surrendered on May 7, 1945, and the war in Europe was over.

After 511 days of combat, the Thunderbirds of the 45th Division returned to the United States in September, a month after victory over Japan was declared. The Thunderbirds assembled at Camp Bowie, Texas, to begin deactivation. A year later the division was reorganized as part of the Oklahoma National Guard.

Once he came home to the United States, Lieutenant Montgomery underwent multiple surgeries. Doctors were uncertain if he would ever be able to walk again.

Dachau inmates greeting U.S. troops, 1945

Montgomery receives the Medal of Honor in January 1945 from President Franklin Roosevelt.

After a lengthy recovery, Montgomery returned to active duty and was sent to Camp Wolters in Texas in late 1944. He had over thirty inches of scars caused by the shrapnel, some of it still in his body.

While at Camp Wolters, he received a letter from the company clerk asking if he had received his Medal of Honor. Montgomery was puzzled but paid it little mind until he was summoned to the White House. On January 15, 1945, President Franklin Roosevelt presented Lieutenant Jack C. Montgomery with the nation's highest military honor. His mother and siblings were in attendance. Montgomery later remembered his nervousness standing next to the president's desk in the

An Allied soldier inspects the graves of his comrades at Anzio in March 1944. Over a hundred thousand Allied soldiers and sailors were killed or wounded during the Anzio campaign.

Oval Office: "I bet my fingerprints are still on that desk, I was squeezing it so hard."

After being discharged from the service in September, Jack Montgomery returned to Oklahoma. For many years, he worked for the Veterans Administration in Muskogee and other nearby towns.

In addition to the Medal of Honor, Montgomery was also the recipient of the Silver Star Medal for valor and two Purple Hearts in recognition of being twice wounded in action (he had also been hit by German shrapnel during the Salerno campaign in late 1943). Always modest, Montgomery spoke very little of his exploits on the battlefield. One day, the woman he would

THUNDERBIRD HONORS

Lieutenant Jack C. Montgomery was not the only Medal of Honor winner from the 45th Division. The unit was highly decorated:

Medals of Honor	8
Distinguished Service Crosses	61
Distinguished Service Medals	3
Silver Star Medals	1,848
Legions of Merit	38
Soldier's Medals	59
Bronze Star Medals	5,744
Air Medals	52
Distinguished Unit Citations	7

soon marry noticed something hanging on his office wall and asked him what it was. He dismissed it with, "Oh, that's just something I did back during in the war." That something was his Medal of Honor.

"I was just doing the job I was supposed to be doing," he would say whenever the subject of his medal came up. Like most of those who are decorated with a Medal of Honor, he didn't consider himself heroic. The heroes were the ones who didn't come home. "I got lucky," he said.

Jack C. Montgomery passed away on June 11, 2002, in Muskogee, Oklahoma, at the age of eighty-four. Today, the Veterans Affairs medical center in Muskogee is named in his honor.

Semper Anticus.

Always Forward.

JACK C. MONTGOMERY'S MEDAL OF HONOR CITATION

THE UNITED STATES OF AMERICA

TO ALL WHO SHALL SEE THESE PRESENTS, GREETING:
THIS IS TO CERTIFY THAT
THE PRESIDENT OF THE UNITED STATES OF AMERICA
PURSUANT TO ACTS OF CONGRESS APPROVED MARCH 3, 1863
AND JULY 9, 1918, HAS AWARDED IN THE NAME OF CONGRESS
TO FIRST LIEUTENANT JACK C. MONTGOMERY,
INFANTRY, UNITED STATES ARMY

THE MEDAL OF HONOR

FOR CONSPICUOUS GALLANTRY AND INTREPIDITY INVOLVING
RISK OF LIFE ABOVE AND BEYOND THE CALL OF DUTY
IN ACTION WITH THE ENEMY
NEAR PADIGLIONE, ITALY, 22 FEBRUARY 1944

For conspicuous gallantry and intrepidity at risk of life above and beyond the call of duty on 22 February 1944, near Padiglione, Italy. Two hours before daybreak a strong force of enemy infantry established themselves in 3 echelons at 50 yards, 100 yards, and 300 yards, respectively, in front of the rifle platoons commanded by 1st Lt. Montgomery. The closest position, consisting of 4 machineguns and 1 mortar, threatened the immediate security of the platoon position. Seizing an M1 rifle and several hand grenades, 1st. Lt. Montgomery crawled up a ditch to within hand grenade range of the enemy. Then climbing boldly onto a little mound, he fired his rifle and threw his grenades so accurately that he killed 8 of the enemy and captured the remaining 4. Returning to his platoon, he called for artillery fire on a house, in and around which he suspected that the majority of the enemy had entrenched themselves. Arming himself with a carbine, he proceeded along the shallow ditch, as withering fire from the riflemen and machinegunners in the second position was concentrated on him. He attacked this position with such fury that 7 of the enemy surrendered to him, and both machineguns were silenced. Three German dead were found in the vicinity later that morning. 1st Lt. Montgomery continued boldly toward the house, 300 yards from his platoon position. It was now daylight, and the enemy observation was excellent across the flat open terrain which led to 1st Lt. Montgomery's objective. When the artillery barrage had lifted, 1st Lt. Montgomery ran fearlessly toward the strongly defended position. As the enemy started streaming out of the house, 1st Lt. Montgomery, unafraid of treacherous snipers, exposed himself daringly to assemble the surrendering enemy and send them to the rear. His fearless, aggressive, and intrepid actions that morning, accounted for a total of 11 enemy dead, 32 prisoners, and an unknown number of wounded. That night, while aiding an adjacent unit to repulse a counterattack, he was struck by mortar fragments and seriously wounded. The selflessness and courage exhibited by 1st Lt. Montgomery in alone attacking 3 strong enemy positions inspired his men to a degree beyond estimation.

KEY TERMS AND NAMES

Allies The countries that banded together to defeat Hitler and the other Axis powers. The main Allied powers were Great Britain, France, the Soviet Union, China, and the United States, but the Allies comprised forty-six countries who were wartime members of the United Nations.

Axis powers Germany, Italy, and Japan. The term comes from the Rome-Berlin Axis agreement signed by Germany and Italy in 1936. It grew to include Japan when the three countries made a defensive alliance in 1940.

Balkans Mountainous peninsula of southeastern Europe comprised of several countries, including Bulgaria, Romania, and Greece.

Battle of Britain The Royal Air Force's defense against the intense bombing of Great Britain by Nazi Germany from July to September 1940.

blitzkrieg A violent surprise offensive by massed air and ground forces. It comes from the German *Blitz* (lightning) and *Krieg* (war).

chancellor Germany's head of government. Germany also has a president, who is the head of state, representing the country in ceremonies at home and abroad.

Churchill, Winston (1874–1965) The prime minister of Great Britain during World War II.

commission An official document issued by a government giving the recipient the rank of an officer in the armed forces.

communism A political doctrine derived from the philosophy of Karl Marx (1818–83), advocating the overthrow of the wealthy by the poor and leading to a society in which all property is publicly owned and each person works and is paid according to ability and need.

counterintelligence Spy tactics designed to deceive and sabotage the enemy.

Dust Bowl The farming area of the Great Plains, including the panhandle of Oklahoma, that suffered severe drought in the early 1930s. With no native grasses to hold the soil in place, winds carried it away in huge dust storms that sometimes reached the East Coast.

Eisenhower, Dwight D. (1890–1969) The supreme commander of the Allied forces in Europe. General Eisenhower oversaw the invasions of North Africa, Sicily, and Salerno, Italy, before directing the Normandy invasion. He was president of the United States from 1953 to 1961.

Fleming, Ian (1908–64) British writer who worked in Naval Intelligence during World War II and went on to write novels featuring the spy James Bond, Agent 007. He also wrote the children's story *Chitty Chitty Bang Bang.*

Great Depression A worldwide economic downturn that started after a huge decline in the stock market on Black Tuesday, October 29, 1929. The United States suffered extreme economic distress until it increased manufacturing and industrial output in the years prior to entering World War II.

Gustav Line The main German defensive line that ran for a hundred miles through the mountains across the narrowest part of the Italian Peninsula, blocking the route to Rome from the south.

Hitler, Adolf (1889–1945) Leader of Germany from 1933 to 1945. On April 30, 1945, two days before the Soviet army took control of Berlin, he took his own life.

M1 rifle The most commonly used rifle by U.S. forces in World War II. The light, semiautomatic rifle could fire about nine hundred rounds a minute.

Montgomery, Bernard (1887–1976) Commander who led British, Canadian, and Australian forces in North Africa, Sicily, and Italy before he was recalled to plan and lead forces in the Normandy invasion.

Mussolini, Benito (1883–1945) The dictator of Italy from 1922 to 1943 and an ally of Hitler. After the daring rescue in 1943, Hitler installed Mussolini as head of a puppet government in the north of Italy. Italian communists executed him on April 28, 1945.

naval attaché A naval officer appointment to work with diplomats in foreign countries.

Nazi Party The National Socialist German Workers' Party. Led by Adolf Hitler, the party stressed the obedience of German citizens to the government in all matters and emphasized inequality of the races.

Nebelwerfer A six-tube German rocket launcher that could propel shells more than three miles. Because of the shells' screeching sound, U.S. and British troops nicknamed them Moaning Minnies and Screaming Mimis.

Operation Husky The code name for the amphibious assault by Allied armies on Sicily, which began July 9, 1943.

Operation Overlord The code name for the amphibious assault by the Allied forces on the the north coast of France, June 6, 1944. The Normandy landing is known as D-Day, but the start date of any military operation is called D-Day.

Operation Shingle The code name for the Allies' amphibious assault on Anzio, Italy, which began January 22, 1944.

Patton, George S. (1885–1945) Commander of U.S. forces in the invasion of Sicily and the leader of the U.S. Third Army's advance across northern France after D-Day. Known for strict discipline and toughness, the general whipped U.S. troops into shape in North Africa.

rear guard One or more military units assigned to bring up and protect the rear of a main force.

Rommel, Erwin (1891–1944) German field marshal who excelled at desert warfare in North Africa. He earned the open respect of Allied commanders. Hitler forced him to take poison after he was linked to a plot to overthrow the dictator.

Siegfried Line A system of concrete pillboxes and strongpoints stretching along Germany's western border for nearly four hundred miles. It was also called the West Wall. The pillboxes contained machine guns and antitank weapons.

NOTES

13 "There were maybe three": Bean, "Jack C. Montgomery," p. 477.

15 "showed great determination": Bean, p. 477.

18 "Did that little ole boy": Bean, p. 479.

36 "All of them were good": This and the quotation following it are from Bean, p. 477.

42 "A corpse dressed as an airman": Ben Macintyre, *Operation Mincemeat: How a Dead Man and a Bizarre Plan Fooled the Nazis and Assured an Allied Victory* (New York: Harmony, 2010), p. 12.

53 "I took charge of the platoon": Whitlock, *The Rock of Anzio*, p. 96.

54 "The Forty-Fifth Division, a green outfit": Whitlock, p. 53.

57 "the soft underbelly of Europe": Midgley, "Why Churchill Thought."

63 "I was supposed to set up": Whitlock, *Rock of Anzio*, p. 106.

65 "It ain't right": Atkinson, Day of Battle, p. 362.

67 "I had hoped": Reynolds, *In Command of History*, p. 392.

67 "The LST had a flat": Crandall, "Soldier's Personal Account."

71 "The terrain there was kind of flat": Whitlock, *Rock of Anzio*, pp. 243–44.

73 "I was always going": Whitlock, p. 244.

75 "I went over": Whitlock, p. 244.

75 "It wasn't very long": Whitlock, p. 244.

75 "The hospital was just tents": Whitlock, p. 244.

76 "When I got back": Whitlock, p. 244.

79 "I seen thousands": James A. Rose, "Impressions of Dachau," 2004, 1:12 video, Holocaust Encyclopedia, U.S. Holocaust Memorial Museum. encyclopedia.ushmm.org/content/en/oral-history/james -rose-describes-his-impressions-of-dachau-upon-liberation.

82 "I bet my fingerprints": Bean, "Jack C. Montgomery," p. 489.

83 "Oh, that's just something": Martin, "Jack Montgomery."

83 "I was just doing the job": Martin, "Jack Montgomery."

SELECTED BIBLIOGRAPHY

Atkinson, Rick. *The Day of Battle: The War in Sicily and Italy, 1943–1944*. New York: Henry Holt, 2007. This sweeping, brilliantly detailed account of both the Sicily and Italian campaigns takes a broad, overview approach to the story, but excellently lays out the story of each battle, along with the personalities involved in the planning and execution of each campaign.

Bean, Christopher B. "Jack C. Montgomery: A Little Big Man." *Chronicles of Oklahoma* 82, no. 4 (Winter 2004–2005): pp. 476–495. This article is the main source for information about Montgomery's life beyond the military. It highlights his education at Chilocco Indian School, Barcone College, and University of Redlands.

Birtle, Andrew. *Sicily, 1943*. Washington, D.C.: U.S. Army Center for Military History, 1993. One of a series of brochures available on the U.S. Army Center for Military History's website, history.army.mil.

Crandall, Rick. "A Soldier's Personal Account of World War II." July 4, 2000. rickcrandall.net/a-soldiers-personal-account-of-world-war-ii/.

D'Este, Carlo. *Fatal Decision: Anzio and the Battle for Rome*. New York: Harper Perennial, 2008. Details the Anzio invasion, the break of the Gustav Line, and the push to the Italian capital.

The 45th: The Story of the 45th Infantry Division. Paris: Stars and Stripes, 1945. lonesentry.com/gi_stories_booklets/45thinfantry/index.html. This booklet, created by *Stars and Stripes*, the official newspaper of the U.S. armed forces, covers the history of the 45th Division. It's an excellent primary source for learning how the soldier in World War II lived and fought on a daily basis.

Martin, Douglas. "Jack Montgomery, 84, and Gino Merli, 78, Two Medal of Honor Winners, Are Dead; Charged Three Enemy Positions at Anzio." *New York Times*, June 17, 2002. nyti.ms/2FUTuIF.

Midgley, Neil. "Why Churchill Thought Attacking Italy Could Win Him World War Two." *Telegraph* (London), Oct. 14, 2012. www .telegraph.co.uk/culture/tvandradio/9598435/Why-Churchill -thought-attacking-Italy-could-win-him-World-War-Two.html.

Ossad, Steve. "Prudence or Paralysis." *WWII History Magazine*, August 2017.

Reynolds, David. *In Command of History: Churchill Fighting and Writing the Second World War*. New York: Random House, 2005.

United States Holocaust Memorial Museum, www.ushmm.org. The museum's digital archive includes video interviews with 45th Infantry soldiers who were involved in the liberation of the Dachau concentration camp in Germany in 1945.

Whitlock, Flint. *The Rock of Anzio: From Sicily to Dachau, A History of the U.S. 45th Infantry Division*. Boulder, CO: Westview, 2005. This definitive history of the Thunderbird Division and its exploits in World War II offers many first-person accounts.